if not sambar, a gravy will do.

Laxmi Vinusha

BookLeaf
Publishing

India | USA | UK

if not sambar, a gravy will do. © 2024
Laxmi Vinusha

Presentation by *BookLeaf Publishing*

Web: www.bookleafpub.com

E-mail: info@bookleafpub.com

ISBN: 9789360943301

First edition 2024

for my Rehana akka,

*your soul in my heart always fills my days with
warmth and love*

PREFACE

Before we dive in, let's set the record straight:
this book has absolutely nothing to do with food.
Nope, not a sprinkle or a crumb. These poems?
Well, they're all just my thoughts about
individuals, family dynamics, and society—no
recipes, haha.

So, why did I put this collection together? Well,
it's a bit of a dream come true, to be honest. Ever
since I cracked open my first book at twelve,
I've been dreaming of putting my own words out
there. This book is my chance to do just that—to
express myself, to let off some steam, and to
hopefully strike a chord with others who've been
down a similar road.

Consider this book a conversation starter, a
chance for us to connect over shared experiences
and emotions. It's my attempt to reach out and
find those who might relate, who might see a
piece of themselves in these pages.

With dosa or anything that goes well with both
sambar and gravy,
Laxmi Vinusha.

I Like It Clumsy

I like my night pants on,
I like to take baths late,
I like to colour my hair and cut it short,
I like my place dishevelled and clumsy,
I'm comfortable with my specs,
And no, I don't mind my pimples
I'm happy with my height and my weight
And I don't think I need to change
If this is luxury, is it even a home?

Traditional Girl

I don't prefer mangalya or sindoor,
I'm allergic to fragrance of flowers,
I would adopt than bear,
I don't want gold jewellery,
It takes comfort for me to smile
I call out insensitive comments

It's not deliberate assassination,
I'm a traditional girl.

"I'm Sorry"

"I don't wanna get married," I said.
I'm sorry, my parents, grandparents,
Uncles and aunts, extended family,
Ancestors, whose names I'm not aware of,
Neighbours and the ex-neighbour
Whose house I went often as a child,
Vegetables vendor and grocery shopkeeper,
Family friends and househelp,

I sincerely apologise for letting you all down.

Heirloom Utensils

My mother received it from her mother,
And my grandmother from hers,
I'll receive it too,
To pass it down to my daughter.
It stays in the storage, gathering dust,
But we never use.

I'm Okay Father

Maybe my silence was too loud,
Maybe I was wistfully staring,
"What happened?" she asked.
"Nothing," I said.
Five minutes with them,
My heart aches, there is a void,
He can never fill.
It's not envy, or is it?

I Believed You

I never knew I was 'dark'
I never knew I was 'skinny'
I never knew I was 'malnourished'
For in my eyes, beauty was me.

Because I believed you
More than anything else,
I saw me through your eyes
Now the vulnerability doesn't hide.

They told me I was dark
That I was 'ugly'
I wouldn't have cried
Had you told me it was a lie.

I wanted to scratch my face
Was ready to bleed,
That way I turned more white,
Feeling whole and complete.

Why didn't you tell me
That I was beautiful?
For I believed you
More than anything else.

Say What You Mean

Boy and girl are the same, you say,
But you say, you are a girl.
I give you freedom, you say,
Why do you "give" me, I ask
I always support your dreams, you say,
I prioritise your happiness, you say,
Fly high, you say,
Limiting the height to the cage.
I spoke to you in my mind, so many times,
I hope to speak for real just once.

What Is Equality To You?

You force me in, and him out,
I'm caged in tradition, he's trapped in doubt.
Both weary and worn, unable to shout.

Stop threatening me with marriage woes,
Let me chase my dreams, my spirit glow,
Beyond the confines of a bridal show.

Stop stifling his spirit before it fully grows,
Let him seek his way, liberated from your gaze,
Trust in his time, he'll traverse the maze.

Both daughter and son, you claim, are the same,
Question the "equality" you so boldly claim,
Is your 'balance' real, or just in name?

Let us make our choices revive,
Let us breathe, grant us room to thrive,
Seeking joy and purpose, let us feel alive.

A Duck

"You shouldn't fly, you're meant to swim,"
They say, but my dreams sigh a hymn.
Not like a vulture, high and wide,
But in my own way, I'll glide.

My wings crave not just for the lake,
But also the sky, my flight to take.
To embrace the clouds, to kiss the sun,
To see the world, to freely run.

If fate confines me to the waves,
I'll seek fresh waters, a new space to trace.
Not bound to one lake, where still waters lie,
In a new domain, beneath expansive skies, I'll
fly.

A Brown Daughter-in-law

Shadows cast by heritage's weight,
A brown daughter finds her fate,
Bound by traditions, smothered breath,
In the echo of ancestral depth.

Suffocating beneath society's gaze,
She yearns to break free from the ancient maze,
For a brown daughter, burdens weigh heavy,
In the silent struggles of cultural levy.

Yet looming still, another chain,
A brown daughter-in-law to feign,
The weight of expectations, heavy and raw,
A role she detests, a path she'd withdraw.

For it doesn't take first-hand to feel the heat,
Of flames that scorch, of fires that fleet,
In the tales of those who've walked before,
She sees the wounds, the scars, the sore.

To be a brown daughter, to be a bride,
Caught in traditions, desperate to hide,
From the flickering flames, the judgments stern,
In the crucible where identities burn.

An Imbalanced Act

"I don't want to get married"
That is all I say,
Can't you love me the same?
Should I choose one?
Can't I have both?

Jewellery? Keep it yourself,
I don't want any.
Saree? Why gather so many?
I have enough already.
Utensils? Oh my god!
First use what's already there.

They don't give a damn about you
They just want to complain
They are looking for a chance.
How come you consider them
But not me?

If Not Sambar, A Gravy Will Do

In a universe where skills galore,
Ukulele strings I never tore,
Nor dance Bharatanatyam's lore,
Nor eloquence in speech did soar,
Yet, these absences, they chose to ignore.

For swimming might guard me against the tide,
And words could armour me in pride,
Dance and music, could save my soul,
Yet, these absences didn't alarm,
As much as my disarray did, they decried.

My disorganised space, a sin so dire,
Sambar's secret, that I'm yet to acquire.
My perspectives, a threat, a menace,
Made me unfit to participate in the race
"A good wife?" They said, making a face.

If not sambar, a gravy will do,
What's the fuss, the unnecessary stew?
My scattered world is not for correction,
In its mess, I find my direction,
My chaos, my satisfaction.

Why seek a man who'd scorn my voice?
Skills can be learned,
A soul can't be tamed,
A good wife, perhaps, I'll never be,
But in my essence, I am truly me.

Ramesh Uncle's Cup of Coffee

Reclined in chair, with a newspaper in hand,
Ramesh sipped his coffee, so refined,
Casually determining fates, off the cuff,
As if he held life's threads, believing it enough.

"Doesn't Kumar have a daughter?" he mused,
"She's at an age, what's her name again?"
"Sundar has a son, still unwed," he said,
In his mind, fate's silent whispers led.

Horoscopes consulted, stars aligned,
No other pair seemed as perfectly assigned!
Arrangements made, formalities complete,
Their marriage sealed, their destinies entreat.

On the wedding day, Ramesh stepped on the stage,
Smiling wide, like the author of their page.
"Guess who brought all this goodness," he proclaimed,
As if he alone had orchestrated their rhyme.

The girl swept into married life,
Struggling to fulfil the "duties" of a wife.

Her dreams surrendered, yet never forgot,
A silent longing for what she sought.

The efforts strained, their souls apart,
Incompatible beats in each other's heart.
She mourned the life she'd never see,
Heartbroken by a destiny not meant to be.

Ceaseless fights, tears shed in despair,
No rescue came, no solace found anywhere.
She wondered, what sin had she committed?
To deserve this fate, so cruelly permitted.

And amidst it all, Ramesh remained,
Casually sipping coffee, fate entertained.
Deciding the destiny of another nameless girl,
"Doesn't Suresh have a daughter?" he said.

The Sisters Of Dominoes

"You have the biggest responsibility now,
Your moves decide if others allow
Their daughters to step out,
So be mindful, don't let 'em down."

I refuse, though.
To let my life's decisions be taken
By how my ancient oak
Utilised her "freedom."

Nor will I carry the weight,
Not mine to hold, of your debate
On letting my budding rose
Lead her life, however it blooms.

Don't sculpt her dreams with my clay
I'm neither a pattern nor a mould.
Leave the chisel to her hand,
For she knows sculpting better.

The Dining Table

There lived an old man.
He raised three sons,
Now they too have kids of their own.
The family became big.

The old man bought a dining table,
Big enough to accommodate
The entire family, to feast
And share stories big and small.

Everyday he looks at it
With desperate and longing eyes,
Waiting for the day
When the table will be filled with life.

One day they all gathered,
And the table was full,
Like the old man had always dreamt.
Only he wasn't there to witness.

Lock and Key

As a kid, I used to play in the street
At night, I see women
Sitting outside their houses
Lost in thoughts, passing time,
Observing closely the passersby.

I sometimes would call them,
Bringing them back to reality
"What did you want to become?"
I would ask them, curiously.

"I wanted to be a dancer."
"I wanted to be a doctor."
"I wanted to be a rich woman."
"I wanted to reach the space."

I didn't understand why they
Weren't what they wanted to be
I didn't understand dreams
I just thought I wouldn't be them.

A Happy Stone

They don't ask why I'm upset
They decide I'm at fault
I was a sponge, sucking up water
But they also threw dirt
It made it rough, pores clogged
Nothing enters now, water or dirt
I'm not upset anymore, I became a stone
And a stone cannot feel anything
Now they throw the stone
Onto the floor, into the water
Often, to test if it breaks
Or any other reaction
They want the stone to smile
But a stone cannot smile.

No Change Is A Change

I'm not thinking about changing this world.
I just think about not being changed by this
world.

I'm not thinking about changing this world.
I just think about changing the world for
someone.

Lazy Ambitious

You are sick, tired, exhausted,
You are also desperate to change
Something for yourself
And maybe for others
Yet you cannot bring yourself
To do what it takes
You say tomorrow
But that's what you have been saying
For years now
It's suffocating,
You really want to do something
But you don't know where to start,
Or what to do,
But you are particular,
You want to do something.

My Little One

My little baby, I know it feels scary,
I want to hug you, never leave your embrace.
People say, "You are wrong." No, they are
wrong.
I know you can't tell what is happening,
For you don't understand it yourself
But trust me, you'll get over it.
No need to rush, you've got time
Make mistakes, be comfortable doing so.
Don't compare yourself with others,
They are wonderful kids, and so are you.
I know, you didn't even know you needed to
hear this,
But I'll tell you nevertheless, it's alright.

Echoes Across The Mirror

You eyed the cake, its sweetness calling,
Yet hesitated, doubts enthralling.
Unnecessary temptation, you reasoned, stalling.

You kept answers within, uncertain,
Scared what if it was not right, once
Said right, regrets filled you in for keeping quiet.

Once unconfident, yet you
Pushed through, learning what's new,
Unlearned, relearned, and grew.

Praise yourself, don't hold back,
Buy that cake, you deserve a snack.
You don't always have to be on the stack.

Focus not solely on tomorrow's quest,
Forget today, and you'll miss life's zest.
Cherish the present, it's when life's best.

Look how far you've come today.
You'll go further the same way
The little you is so proud of you.

Take Me Home

Do I belong
To the shores?
Where waves gently roll,
Or the caves?
Where echoes console
Or the stars?
Where mysteries unfold
Or the mountains?
Where strength stretches bold
Or the clouds?
Where dreams softly weep,
Or the plains?
Where earth secrets heap.

I don't know
Where to go.
Take me home,
Wherever I roam.

What I Want To Be

Let me travel, not as a tourist
But as an explorer,
Not to escape reality,
But to witness it.

Let me meet new people,
learn a new language,
experience a new culture
And grow as a person.

Let me read, about life,
About human history,
About human behaviour,
Everything, fictional and real.

Let me learn a new skill,
Maybe to play guitar,
Or to crochet, maybe
To skate or to debate.

Let me write a word or two,
Maybe even make movies,
Let me ignite people,
To introspect and think.

A Loud Piano

I couldn't feel a thing,
Yet I knew I was fortunate to have you.
Words don't escape me,
But my heart loves you.

I used to measure my every word,
Every action, cautious and careful.
Alone in a crowd, isolated in laughter,
Enveloped by toxic gaze, passing days.

Then you came along,
Letting me experience real friendship.
Time to time, I still wonder
How I ended up being special to you.

The transition was silent, almost unseen.
Suddenly, I was lucky,
Suddenly, I was myself,
Suddenly, I mattered to someone.

Promise To Come With Me

The forest keeps calling you
I know it's urging you to visit,
But forget it, for now, my friend
Let's go to the meadows instead.
I want to walk across them
I don't want to go alone though
I heard there might be thorns
Maybe, I'm scared, unlike you
I know you'll protect me,
So accompany me, my dear friend
Looking forward to seeing
The butterflies and blooms,
Tomorrow with you.

ACKNOWLEDGEMENT

Hey there,

As I got a chance, I might as well mention a bunch of people.

Harini, thank you for being my unofficial editor-in-chief and official creditor! Your timely financial contribution made the aesthetics of this collection possible. Your critical thoughts and reflective feedback gave me the confidence to trust in the coherence of my words and the strength of my voice.

Much appreciation for Devi, as much as I fancy being a writer, I don't know how long I would have taken for its fruition had you not asked me to publish my poems right away. (/Internal Joke/ You have more HUMANITY than anyone else, haha).

Sneha and Dharshu, who have been stuck with me since forever; we have witnessed different versions of ourselves; thank you for staying with me in all my versions.

I'm forever grateful to the Centre for Women's Studies, Ann Ma'am, Bharathi Akka, Kalyani Akka, Anu and all my "Uliyin-Oli" club members, most coolest people to work with (I apologise for not being able to mention each one of you individually, this page doesn't suffice, but my heart does). I've challenged myself to try various things, learned and evolved as a better person, all thanks to the family I found here. I'll always carry the legacy of our club wherever I go.

I thank my amma, for she gave me some money for graduating high school asking me to buy myself things. You might have wondered how I spent it, well, here it is. Thanks for unknowingly taking part in bankrolling this book.

It's always an incredible feeling to witness someone's growth, whether it's personal development or decision-making. Hepshi and Mythili, I couldn't be more proud of you both.

Prithika and Thangam, you've brought so much into my life, from incredible experiences to invaluable lessons. I'm truly grateful for everything.

Maimoona, Vanaja and Jaya Shruthi, eternal
love for all the positive energy you people
always bring my way.

Swetha, Sudharshini and Shivani *kutta*, always
thankful for your quiet presence and dependable
support.

I can't forget to mention my ELSA
gang—Eniya, Akshya and Shivani—for I shared
my desire to become a writer after reading a
book for the first time in life during 8th grade.
They were very supportive and enthusiastic to
read my creation (sorry, you people had to wait
for 7 years, haha).

Heartfelt thanks to all my friends, family and
well wishers. Wish I could shout out each of you
individually, but hey, you know I keep y'all in
mind, right?

A little nod to cheesecake, for it first melts into
my mouth and eventually manages to melt my
heart, every single time (like seriously!).

A heartfelt gratitude to BookLeaf Publishing for
making my published writer dream a reality.

Leaving the deepest gratitude for last, it might
not always be easy to pick up a book by a new
writer. Since you are here, it means you have
picked up mine. Thank you for holding my
collection and giving my words a chance to
touch a tiny part of you. Sending my love to all
those tiny parts that I could reach.

With a heart full of love
and a mind full of cheesecake,

Laxmi Vinusha <3